Henry Purcell
1659 – 1695

A Purcell Suite

7 Pieces for Descant Recorder and Keyboard
7 Stücke für Sopranblockflöte und Klavier

Edited by / Herausgegeben von
Gwilym Beechey

ED 13218
ISMN 979-0-2201-3086-1

SCHOTT

www.schott-music.com

Mainz · London · Berlin · Madrid · New York · Paris · Prague · Tokyo · Toronto
© 2008 SCHOTT MUSIC Ltd, London · Printed in Germany

ED 13218
British Library Cataloguing-in-Publication Data.
A catalogue record for this book is available from the British Library
ISMN M-2201-3086-1
ISBN 978-1-84761-137-6

© 2008 Schott Music Ltd, London

Music setting by Figaro
Printed in Germany S&Co.8490

Contents

A Purcell Suite

Edited and arranged by/
Herausgegeben und bearbeitet von
Gwilym Beechey

Henry Purcell
(1659–1695)

1. Air in D minor

(King Arthur)

Z 628/3

2. How blest are shepherds

(King Arthur)

Z 628/15

3. Hornpipe in G minor
(*King Arthur*)

Z 628/18

A Purcell Suite

Edited and arranged by/
Herausgegeben und bearbeitet von
Gwilym Beechey

Henry Purcell
(1659–1695)

1. Air in D minor
(King Arthur)

Z 628/3

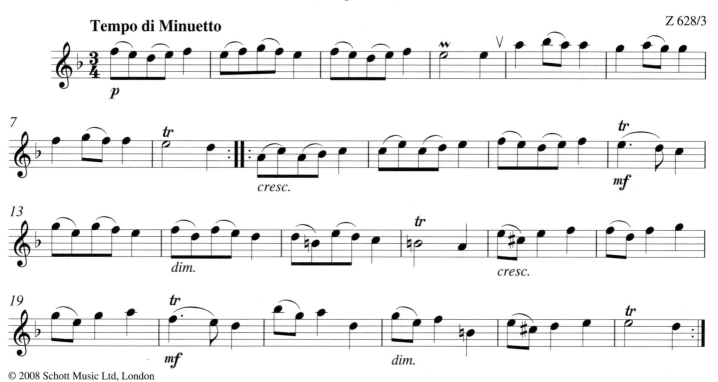

© 2008 Schott Music Ltd, London

2. How blest are shepherds
(King Arthur)

Z 628/15

© 2008 Schott Music Ltd, London

3. Hornpipe in G minor
(*King Arthur*)

Z 628/18

4. Jig in G minor
(*The Fairy Queen*)

Z 629/6

5. Prelude/Minuet in C major

(The Fairy Queen)

Z 629/23

6. Dance in C major

(The Indian Queen)

Z 630/10

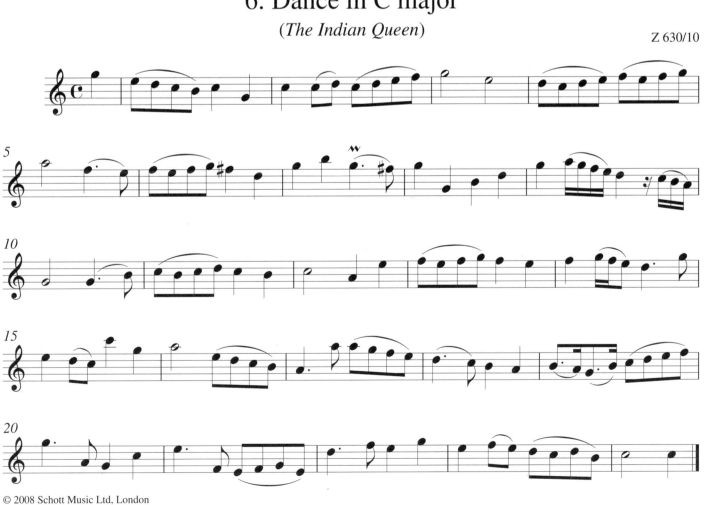

7. Rondeau in D minor

(Abdelazer)

Z 570/2

S&Co.8490 Printed in Germany

4. Jig in G minor
(*The Fairy Queen*)

Z 629/6

Descant Recorder

Keyboard

5. Prelude / Minuet in C major

(The Fairy Queen)

Z 629/23

Descant
Recorder

Keyboard

6. Dance in C major

(The Indian Queen)

Z 630/10

10

7. Rondeau in D minor

(Abdelzer)

Z 570/2

Descant Recorder

Keyboard